Sea Stars

by Lola M. Schaefer

Consulting Editor: Gail Saunders-Smith, Ph.D.

Consultant: Jody Byrum, Science Writer,
SeaWorld Education Department

Pebble Books

an imprint of Capstone Press
Mankato, Minnesota

1

Pebble Books are published by Capstone Press
818 North Willow Street, Mankato, Minnesota 56001
http://www.capstone-press.com

Library of Congress Cataloging-in-Publication Data
Schaefer, Lola M., 1950–
    Sea stars/by Lola M. Schaefer.
    p. cm.—(Ocean life)
    Includes bibliographical references (p. 23) and index.
    Summary: Simple text and photographs introduce sea stars, their appearance,
and behavior.
    ISBN 0-7368-0250-9
    1. Starfishes—Juvenile literature. [1. Starfishes.] I. Title. II. Series: Schaefer,
Lola M., 1950–   Ocean life.
QL384.A8S35   1999
593.9'3—dc21

             98-46094
             CIP
             AC

Note to Parents and Teachers

The Ocean Life series supports national science standards for units
on the diversity and unity of life. The series shows that animals
have features that help them live in different environments. This
book describes and illustrates sea stars, their parts, and their prey.
The photographs support early readers in understanding the text.
The repetition of words and phrases helps early readers learn new
words. This book also introduces early readers to subject-specific
vocabulary words, which are defined in the Words to Know section.
Early readers may need assistance to read some words and to use
the Table of Contents, Words to Know, Read More, Internet Sites,
and Index/Word List sections of the book.

Table of Contents

4

Sea stars are
ocean animals.

6

Sea stars are shaped
like stars.

Sea stars have arms
called rays.

Sea stars can have five or more rays.

12

Sea stars can lose rays.

New rays grow.

Sea stars have small feet on each ray.

Sea stars hold on to
rocks with their feet.

Some sea stars eat clams.
Sea stars can open clam
shells with their feet.

Words to Know

clam—an animal that lives inside a shell; sea stars open the shell and eat the clam.

lose—to fail to keep something; a sea star might lose a ray when another animal attacks.

ocean—a large body of salt water

ray—a limb of an animal that works like an arm; sea stars use rays to move and to hold food.

Read More

Cooper, Jason. *Sea Stars.* Vero Beach, Fla.: Rourke Publications, 1996.

Perry, Phyllis Jean. *Sea Stars and Dragons.* New York: Franklin Watts, 1996.

Stefoff, Rebecca. *Starfish.* Living Things. New York: Benchmark Books, 1997.

Internet Sites

Natural Perspective: Starfish
http://www.perspective.com/nature/animalia/starfish.html

Pictures of Echinoderms
http://www.isl.net/~helf/echino/images.html

The Sea Star
http://www.icon.portland.or.us/education/mbridge/wow/aqua/tidepool/seastar/seastar.htm

Index/Word List

Word Count: 63
Early-Intervention Level: 7

Editorial Credits
Martha E. Hillman, editor; Steve Christensen, cover designer and illustrator;
    Kimberly Danger and Sheri Gosewisch, photo researchers

Photo Credits
Dwight Kuhn, cover
Tom Stack and Associates/Dave B. Fleetham, 1; Mike Severns, 4; Brian Parker, 8, 12,
    16, 18; Mark Newman, 10; Ed Robinson, 14; Gary Milburn, 20
The Wildlife Collection/Chris Huss, 6

DATE DUE